A Note From Denise Renner

The Word of God is so powerful in our lives. It is essential that every person spend time with God and study His Word in order to stay spiritually strong in these last days.

This study guide corresponds to my *TIME With Denise Renner* TV program by the same title that can be viewed at **deniserenner.org**. My desire is that through these lessons, you find the encouragement and freedom in Christ that you need. I believe the Holy Spirit is going to speak to you through the words you read in this study tool and that as you begin to use it, you will be *propelled* into the abundant life God has planned for you. I encourage you to make the effort to receive all He has for you and all He wants to do in you — it will definitely be worth it!

Whether you have walked with the Lord a long time or have just begun to follow Him, there is so much He wants to give you from His Word. He sees where you are, and He wants to meet you there.

Therefore do not worry about tomorrow, for tomorrow will worry about its own things. Sufficient for the day is its own trouble.
Matthew 6:34

Your sister and friend in Jesus Christ,

Denise Renner

God Is On Your Side

1814 W. Tacoma St.
Broken Arrow, Oklahoma 74012

Published by Rick Renner Ministries
www.renner.org

ISBN 13: 978-1-6675-0405-6

eBook ISBN 13: 978-1-6675-0406-3

LESSON 1

TOPIC

'Is God Too Busy To Help Me?'

SCRIPTURES

1. **Isaiah 40:11** — He will feed His flock like a shepherd; He will gather the lambs with His arm, and carry them in His bosom, and gently lead those who are with young.
2. **Isaiah 40:13** — Who has directed the Spirit of the Lord, or as His counselor has taught Him?
3. **Isaiah 40:18-20** — To whom then will you liken God? Or what likeness will you compare to Him? The workman molds an image, the goldsmith overspreads it with gold, and the silversmith casts silver chains. Whoever is too impoverished for such a contribution chooses a tree that will not rot; he seeks for himself a skillful workman to prepare a carved image that will not totter.
4. **Isaiah 40:21-23** — Have you not known? Have you not heard? Has it not been told you from the beginning? Have you not understood from the foundations of the earth? It is He who sits above the circle of the earth, and its inhabitants are like grasshoppers, who stretches out the heavens like a curtain, and spreads them out like a tent to dwell in. He brings the princes to nothing; He makes the judges of the earth useless.
5. **Isaiah 40:25,26** — "To whom then will you liken Me, or to whom shall I be equal?" says the Holy One. Lift up your eyes on high, and see who has created these things, who brings out their host by number; He calls them all by name, by the greatness of His might and the strength of His power; not one is missing.
6. **Isaiah 40:31** — But those who wait on the Lord shall renew their strength; they shall mount up with wings like eagles, they shall run and not be weary, they shall walk and not faint.

SYNOPSIS

Waiting on the Lord is an important part of the Christian life. In fact, the Bible teaches us that waiting on the Lord is the key to receiving His power and strength. But many Christians often wonder what this practice looks like and question if God really cares about their daily needs. While God is magnificent and all-powerful, He is at the same time a loving Shepherd who takes care of His little lambs. Not only does He have the ability and strength to help us when we need Him, He also longs to help us when we call out to Him. By waiting on the Lord, we can draw close to Him and receive all He has for us!

The emphasis of this lesson:

Learning to wait on the Lord is one of the most important things you can do in your spiritual walk. Although it requires patience, transparency, and humility, waiting on the Lord can release God's power and strength into your life. When you understand both the magnificence and tender care of God's character, you will recognize that He is just the Person who has what you need — and who wants to give it to you in fullness. By acknowledging God in your daily life, you can accomplish more than ever before because He will give you the wisdom, strength, and power you need for the task at hand.

Waiting on the Lord

Waiting is something most people have had to do at some point in their lives. Many people have had to wait on their spouse or children to change. Some women have had to wait to get married or to have a baby, while others have had to wait on different opportunities or for the season of life they're in to change. In any case, waiting is not always easy, and it requires us to have much patience in the process.

When it comes to waiting on the Lord and His appropriate timing in our lives, we need to seek God's wisdom and counsel. Thankfully, the Bible is full of admonition to guide our steps during these seasons of process. By studying the Word, we can find encouragement, strength, and direction that will lead us properly through times that may not seem so enjoyable to our flesh.

One of the most well-known scriptures regarding waiting is found in Isaiah 40:31: "But those who wait on the Lord shall renew their strength; they shall mount up with wings like eagles, they shall run and not be weary, they shall walk and not faint." What a promise to hold on to in those dry or slow places of life! When we learn to wait upon the Lord, we will be strengthened in our hearts and prepared to run our race victoriously.

While we wait on the Lord, we are also listening to Him to understand His opinion and instruction about every situation. He then empowers us to take the right steps and make the right decisions according to His perfect timing and plan. Our ability to wait on God is essential!

Understanding the Magnificence of God

God longs for us to wait on Him and hear what He has to say to our hearts. He wants us to receive what He has to give us. He is not dull of hearing, and He is attentive to our prayers. Unlike false gods, He's not going to topple over with a big crash. Nothing takes Him by surprise! (*See* Isaiah 40:21-23.)

God is not intimidated by any government, prince, or judge because He is so much more powerful than any man or institution. The Bible says He stretches out the heavens like a curtain. He's so massive and can do the impossible!

Isaiah 40:25 and 26 tells us that God is unparalleled. No one is His equal, nor can anything be compared to Him. He is the Creator of the Heavens and is full of might and power. Not even the most talented scientist with the most powerful telescope can see as far as God sees in the universe. He notices every single star in all the galaxies of space and makes sure not one is missing. He is holding creation up by the power of His hand.

This is the magnificence of the God we serve! The power He uses to uphold the universe is the same power He uses to heal a broken bone or sick body. The Bible tells us Jesus was touched with the feelings of our infirmities. And as all-powerful as God is, He also cares about the little details in our lives.

God possesses infinite wisdom and desires to share it with us when we ask. He is not deaf like idols made of wood and stone; He is alive and listening to our prayers. Isaiah 40:13 and 14 reveals the magnitude of God's glorious wisdom. No one has ever needed to teach Him anything because He is the source of all wisdom, knowledge, and understanding, and that's almost too much for our minds to conceive!

Understanding the Shepherd's Heart of God

We have established that God cannot be exceeded in power or greatness, but the Bible attributes another outstanding quality to Him that makes Him very personable. This character trait is His heart of a Shepherd toward us.

Isaiah 40:11 says, "He will feed His flock like a shepherd…." In His vastness of power and might, the Lord is also tender and caring in His watchfulness over us. Ultimately, He is the One in charge of our lives and the One who feeds us. We are the sheep of His pasture, and He knows us each by name.

Verse 11 also says that God gathers the lambs with His arm. He doesn't condemn us or beat us up when we go astray. Rather, He gathers us up in His tender mercy and brings us close to His heart.

This is a beautiful reminder of how the Lord cares for those who are lost or backslidden. As we're praying for loved ones who are not walking with the Lord, we can trust the Great Shepherd to pull them back into place and gather them into His arms. He is the God who leaves the 99 and goes after that one who is lost or wounded.

Isaiah 40:11 goes on to say that God will "…carry them in His bosom, and gently lead those who are with young." God doesn't want His sheep far away from Him. Because He carries us so close to His heart, He desires to impart strength to us when we are weak or burdened down by life.

When we get busy or overworked with our different responsibilities, we need to remember that our Good Shepherd is holding us close to His heart. He's carrying us. It's by His grace that we can open our eyes every morning and accomplish the tasks at hand.

By drawing close to God, we give Him an opportunity to fill us with His strength and His wisdom. When we come into situations that we don't know how to handle, we can draw from the wisdom of God. The Holy Spirit can tell us how to proceed and what to do or not do if we will just stay close to Him.

As we grow in our walk with God, He remains patient with us just like a Shepherd with little lambs. He leads us gently; He's not beating us into submission or obedience. The Bible refers to the Holy Spirit as our "comforter" — He doesn't condemn us but teaches us the right way to go.

Renewed With Strength

In its simplest terms, waiting on the Lord is just acknowledging His presence. It's recognizing that our strength comes from the Lord. He is the source of our life and our breath. He's the One who created everything about us — our minds, our bodies, our hearts, our lungs — and He is the One who can fill us with peace every single moment of every day.

When we acknowledge God for who He is and what He's done for us, He begins to renew our strength. We need His energy and power to move throughout the day. Thankfully, He's not stingy with His resources! God loves to pour out on us whatever we need from Him. He comes to us with an open hand, not a clenched fist.

In our waiting on God and acknowledging Him, we can confess to the Lord our shortcomings and human inabilities. We are able to recognize that we cannot do things on our own and that we need His strength, wisdom, and help. Our willingness to be open and transparent before the Lord gives Him an invitation to help us and infuse us with His supernatural strength.

Waiting on the Lord is an important discipline we need to develop in our walk with God. While God is so magnificent and powerful, He is at the same time a loving and caring Father. Just like a Shepherd who watches over His flock, God cares for us. He longs to draw us close and impart His strength into us when we simply wait upon Him.

STUDY QUESTIONS

Study to shew thyself approved unto God, a workman that needeth not to be ashamed, rightly dividing the word of truth.
— 2 Timothy 2:15

1. Isaiah 40:31 says, "But those who wait on the Lord shall renew their strength; they shall mount up with wings like eagles, they shall run and not be weary, they shall walk and not faint." Think of a time when you put this Scripture into practice. How did God renew your strength while you waited on Him?

2. Isaiah 40:25 and 26 tells us that God is unparalleled. Take a moment to meditate on the greatness of God. What aspect of His magnificence stands out to you most?
3. Isaiah 40:11 depicts God's tender heart of a Shepherd. Do you often think of God as your Shepherd?

PRACTICAL APPLICATION

But be ye doers of the word, and not hearers only,
deceiving your own selves.
—James 1:22

1. Do you take time to regularly wait upon the Lord?
2. When you are praying for others, do you get worried or anxious about their situations, or do you trust God the Good Shepherd to take care of them?
3. What situations are you facing today that seem overwhelming to you? Have you acknowledged your limitations before God and asked Him to help you?

LESSON 2

TOPIC

'Is There Help for Me To Get My Strength Back?'

SCRIPTURES

1. **Isaiah 40:31** — But those who wait on the Lord shall renew their strength; they shall mount up with wings like eagles, they shall run and not be weary, they shall walk and not faint.
2. **Joshua 14:11,12**— As yet I am as strong this day as on the day that Moses sent me; just as my strength was then, so now is my strength for war, both for going out and for coming in. Now therefore, give me this mountain of which the Lord spoke in that day; for you heard in that day how the Anakim were there, and that the cities were great

and fortified. It may be that the Lord will be with me, and I shall be able to drive them out as the Lord said.

3. **Deuteronomy 34:7** — Moses was one hundred and twenty years old when he died. His eyes were not dim nor his natural vigor diminished.
4. **Philippians 1:6** — Being confident of this very thing, that He who has begun a good work in you will complete it until the day of Jesus Christ.
5. **Hebrews 12:2** — Looking unto Jesus, the author and finisher of our faith, who for the joy that was set before Him endured the cross, despising the shame, and has sat down at the right hand of the throne of God.
6. **Romans 8:11** — But if the Spirit of Him who raised Jesus from the dead dwells in you, He who raised Christ from the dead will also give life to your mortal bodies through His Spirit who dwells in you.
7. **Job 23:14** — For He performs what is appointed for me, and many such things are with Him.
8. **2 Timothy 4:7** — I have fought the good fight, I have finished the race, I have kept the faith.

SYNOPSIS

The Bible promises that those who wait upon the Lord shall renew their strength. In both the Old and New Testament, we see examples of people who defied the odds by connecting with God's grace, strength, and ability. Many even accomplished great tasks in their older years through an infusion of God's supernatural strength. By learning to wait on the Lord and receive from His resources of power and grace, we can continue pressing forward in God's plans for us — even in our older years of life.

The emphasis of this lesson:

No matter what season of life we are in, our strength can be renewed by the power of God. According to Isaiah 40:31, the secret to obtaining that supernatural strength comes from waiting on the Lord. From the examples of Moses, Caleb, and the apostle John, we learn how God's strength empowered old men to finish their races strong. By activating our faith, we can also receive God's strength to live out a long, healthy life and to complete our assignment on the earth.

Strength Comes From Waiting on the Lord

Do you need your strength renewed? Like most people, you have probably experienced times when you felt weak, discouraged, tired, exhausted, or worn out. Perhaps your energy levels just felt depleted, or you were emotionally drained by extenuating circumstances. Maybe you've even taken vitamins or special energy drinks just to regain some of your vigor and strength.

While it's important for us to take care of our bodies with vitamins, exercise, and a healthy diet, natural things have limits in helping us rebuild our strength. Thankfully, the Bible gives us a promise of supernatural strength and encouragement! Isaiah 40:31 declares, "...Those who wait on the Lord shall renew their strength...." Our God who has unlimited strength and power is able to infuse us with His strength when we learn to wait upon Him.

Biblical and Modern-Day Examples of People Who Received Strength From God

The Bible is full of individuals who were supernaturally empowered by the strength of God. For example, Caleb displayed extraordinary strength in his old age. Joshua 14 tells us that Caleb was ready to possess the land and take on a mountain when he was 85 years old!

Similarly, Moses remained strong well into his hundreds. Deuteronomy 34:7 says, "Moses was one hundred and twenty years old when he died. His eyes were not dim nor his natural vigor diminished." At the time of his death at age 120, Moses still had strength in his body. Only God's supernatural power could have preserved his health and body like that.

As we age, we don't have to receive negative reports that say we will become weaker and weaker or that we'll have to see a doctor more and more. God can keep us strong and healthy all throughout our lives, even when we grow older. That is the promise of life we have in Him. We can believe that our bodies will be strong, our eyes will not grow dim, our bones will be healthy, and our minds will stay sharp as long as we allow the Lord to renew our strength.

Because Caleb and Moses lived in the Old Testament, they didn't even have the Holy Spirit living inside them like we do today. Can you imagine how much more strength and might we can receive as new creatures in Christ through the indwelling Spirit of God? The very power of God is living on the inside of us!

Another biblical example of someone who received strength in their old age was the apostle John. Historians say that John was 95 when he received the revelation that later became the book of Revelation in the Bible. Obviously, God didn't view him as useless, helpless, or outdated in his old age. Rather, God revealed Jesus as the Resurrected Christ to John in his elderly years. It is even believed that John continued to encourage and strengthen the brethren of the Church until the day he died.

The power that was resident in the apostle John is the same power that is still at work inside us today. God's power is available to strengthen us, renew us, and keep us healthy. Even in our old age, we can be strong in the Lord and in the power of His might!

A modern-day example of someone who has walked in the strength of God is Kenneth Copeland. Although he is older now, Brother Copeland continues to travel, preach, sing, and record in his studio. His age hasn't stopped him one bit — in fact, he recently started a Bible school while in his eighties. Thanks to the power of God quickening him, he is still a man *full* of vigor and strength.

No matter how old we become, we can continue moving forward in God's plan on earth. Someone in their sixties who may be nearing retirement can start a brand-new business. Grandparents can pour their lives into children and youth. A 70-year-old can lead a discipleship group in church. As long as we are looking to the Lord to infuse us with His strength, we can keep running our race to the finish line.

God's Spirit Is Active

The Bible tells us in Isaiah 40 that those who wait on God will never faint or become weary — God is the same way! He is constantly moving and active. Therefore, the Holy Spirit within you is also always active. He never stops working in you, providing you with supernatural strength, energy, wisdom, and ability.

Philippians 1:6 says, "Being confident of this very thing, that He who has begun a good work in you will complete it until the day of Jesus Christ." Just because God started something in you many years ago doesn't mean

He is finished with you now. Like the Bible promises, He will continue developing, growing, maturing, molding, and teaching you until that glorious day when Jesus Christ returns.

As God works out the plan of salvation in your life and brings it to completion, He's moving you forward. And as a result, mercy and grace will continue to abound toward you, enabling you to fulfill God's plan. By cooperating with the Holy Spirit's activity in your life, you can remain resilient, steadfast, and strong throughout all your years.

Because God is eternal, His supernatural power and activity never cease. The Bible even says His mercies and compassions are new every morning, which means this is a daily activity! God is not passive in His dealings with us — He remains very active, constantly supplying us with His resources every day.

Hebrews 12:2 reminds us that Jesus is also the author and finisher of our faith. This is another picture of God's constant activity in our life. He's moving us from one place to another and bringing us to the finish line.

Along the same lines, Romans 8:11 says, "But if the Spirit of Him who raised Jesus from the dead dwells in you, He who raised Christ from the dead will also give life to your mortal bodies through His Spirit who dwells in you." The Holy Spirit is completely active and is the One giving life to our mortal bodies. He's quickening us to have strength today. He's infusing us with power to keep our minds sharp and our bodies strong.

Whatever our assignment is in life, we can rest assured God has equipped us for the task. Job 23:14 says, "For He performs what is appointed for me…." This means that God is enabling us to carry out what He's given us to do. God is empowering mothers to raise their babies. He's equipping women to help their husbands. He's strengthening businesspeople to do their jobs. And as we go through our days working on the tasks at hand, God is performing through us what is appointed for us. His Spirit is not passive in our lives — He is *active*!

In light of God's active nature, we can also be active in our own faith. This means that we are not passively waiting for something to happen or dreaming of "one day" or "someday" to come. Rather, we are actively believing God every day — taking Him at His Word, confessing it with our mouths, and obeying it with our actions. No matter how difficult things become, we are refusing to quit or draw back from actively trusting in the Lord.

Paul the apostle was a great example of someone who actively lived in faith. Although he encountered great difficulty along the way, he refused to give up. He continued pressing forward in his ministry assignment until the task was complete. In Second Timothy 4:7, he wrote: "I have fought the good fight, I have finished the race, I have kept the faith." Paul was able to accomplish all that he did by the grace of God and by living a lifestyle of active faith.

We can be encouraged by Paul's testimony of overcoming adversity through his faith in God. Paul connected with the activity of God's Spirit — His grace, strength, power, wisdom, provision, and protection — and received what he needed to fulfill his assignment. Similarly, we can also overcome every obstacle in our life by partnering with God's activity in our life. As He is active to pour out His resources of grace and power, we can actively receive from Him by our faith. When we connect with God's supernatural activity with active faith, we will be able to stay in the race until the end. Just like Paul, we can then look back on our lives and say, "I have fought the good fight, I have finished the race, and I have kept the faith."

STUDY QUESTIONS

Study to shew thyself approved unto God, a workman that needeth not to be ashamed, rightly dividing the word of truth.
— 2 Timothy 2:15

1. Isaiah 40:31 declares, "...Those who wait on the Lord shall renew their strength...." Can you think of a time in your life when you were strengthened because you waited on the Lord?
2. Deuteronomy 34:7 says, "Moses was one hundred and twenty years old when he died. His eyes were not dim nor his natural vigor diminished." Do you know someone who has lived a godly life and still exhibits physical strength in their old age?
3. In Second Timothy 4:7, Paul wrote: "I have fought the good fight, I have finished the race, I have kept the faith." If you were in Paul's shoes, would you have remained active in your faith in the face of hardship, persecution, suffering, and shipwrecks so that you could finish your race?

PRACTICAL APPLICATION

**But be ye doers of the word, and not hearers only,
deceiving your own selves.
—James 1:22**

1. Take a moment to reflect on God's activity in your life. What are some of His resources you are thankful for today?
2. What difficulties are obstructing your path? How are you actively living your faith to overcome these obstacles?
3. When you think of growing older, do you see yourself limited by age or empowered by the Holy Spirit?

LESSON 3

TOPIC

'Is It Possible To Fly Higher?'

SCRIPTURES

1. **Isaiah 40:31** — But those who wait on the Lord shall renew their strength; they shall mount up with wings like eagles, they shall run and not be weary, they shall walk and not faint.
2. **Isaiah 54:2** — Enlarge the place of your tent, and let them stretch out the curtains of your dwellings; do not spare; lengthen your cords, and strengthen your stakes.

SYNOPSIS

The Bible teaches that those who wait upon the Lord shall mount up with wings like eagles. A powerful bird of prey, an eagle is created by divine design to gracefully ride on the winds of a storm. By better understanding the abilities of an eagle, we can learn how the Holy Spirit supernaturally strengthens us to soar over adversity in peace and joy.

The emphasis of this lesson:

Waiting on the Lord enables us to overcome difficulties with the power and strength of the Holy Spirit. Like an eagle, we can fly high above the

winds of life and take authority over the attacks of the enemy. As we learn from Denise's personal story, we will see that we have authority over our own personal thoughts and emotions. No matter what season of life we are in, we can choose the fruit of the Spirit over resentment and depression!

Fly Like an Eagle

As we have seen in the last few lessons, the Bible teaches that strength comes when we wait upon the Lord. Isaiah 40:31 states, "But those who wait on the Lord shall renew their strength; they shall mount up with wings like eagles...." God's supernatural strength can literally lift us up and over any difficulty.

In his book *On Eagles Wings*, Col Stringer described the unique function and capabilities of the eagle. As an accomplished flyer, an eagle can soar above the storms and even cyclonic conditions with mastery of flight. While other birds are thrown by these powerful winds, the eagle actually uses these winds to his advantage. Instead of being blown over and destroyed by the wind, he is built to glide above it. Isn't that amazing?

Another interesting fact about the eagle is the particular construction of his wings. His feathers are tapered at the tips, which form slots that act like shock absorbers. Similar to the shock absorbers in a vehicle, these slots put a barrier between the eagle and the wind so the eagle doesn't feel "road bumps" during his flight. Instead of being knocked over by the power of the wind, the eagle continues to move forward without injury due to the amazing anatomy of his wings.

In the same fashion, we can develop spiritual "shock absorbers" by learning to wait on the Lord. God's strength enables us to overcome any resistance in our journey so we won't feel the "bumps in the road" whenever we are pressed by difficulty. Because of the power of the Holy Spirit, we will rise over those circumstances in peace and joy!

Eagles are also created with the ability to make adjustments mid-flight. An eagle can hover in the sky as steady as a rock while his wing tips move constantly and automatically to adjust to the air currents. This is a powerful picture of how the Holy Spirit helps us make adjustments as we follow Christ.

Whenever the enemy whispers lies in our ears, the Holy Spirit strengthens us to reject those thoughts by helping us adjust our thinking according to the Word of God. If fear tries to bind our minds, the Holy Spirit will remind us that fear doesn't come from God. Should bad reports surround us, the Greater One inside us will keep us steady in the midst of the storm.

As believers full of the power of the Holy Spirit, we don't have to be afraid of life's tests and trials because we have something inside us that will anchor us. We can move through any difficulty with spiritual shock absorbers. Nothing will move or shake us — we will just adjust as the Holy Spirit leads and keep moving forward in victory.

Another characteristic of the eagle is his keen eyesight. In fact, an eagle can see five times better than humans. Similarly, God can give us deep spiritual eyesight that enables us to see things we couldn't have seen on our own. He will show us situations from a different vantage point so we can walk in love, mercy, and truth. Instead of yelling or screaming at others, we can respond to them with compassion and understanding.

Finally, an eagle has a unique ability to come to a powerful stop while swooping down to pick up its prey. About 15 feet away from its target, an eagle will spread out his wings and stretch out his talons. This seamless motion acts like a braking mechanism in a car and demonstrates the eagle's authority to stop when needed.

Likewise, when we acknowledge the Holy Spirit inside us, we can put the brakes on whenever we hear a bad report. We can take our wings of authority to stop fear and doubt from coming into our hearts, and by waiting on the Lord, we can use our strength to do the right thing!

An example of someone who used her "wings of authority" was Queen Esther. When faced with the potential alienation of the Jews, Queen Esther waited on God and submitted to His plan for saving her people. By walking humbly in the authority of her royal position, she put the brakes on the enemy's agenda and preserved an entire nation.

Denise's Personal Story

In relation to the importance of "putting the brakes" on the enemy's plans, Denise shared a personal story from her early years of motherhood. During this time in her life, she was often left home alone to raise three young boys while Rick was traveling for ministry. In his absence, Denise began to feel sorry for herself. As she sought the Lord for an answer, the Lord took her to Isaiah 54:2, which states, "Enlarge the place of your tent, and let them stretch out the curtains of your dwellings; do not spare; lengthen your cords, and strengthen your stakes."

When Denise read that scripture, the Lord showed her two sets of emotions she could choose. On the one side were godly emotions such as peace, love, and joy; on the other side were feelings of anger, depression, sadness, and resentment. By feeling sorry for herself and crying all the time, Denise was allowing the negative set of emotions to rule her life.

As the Lord revealed this, He showed Denise it was time for her to embrace the positive set of emotions. Instead of resenting her husband for being on the road so much, she could choose to be supportive of him. Even though it was a difficult season, the Lord empowered Denise to find joy and peace in her situation. She had the authority to put the brakes on resentment, jealousy, and anger, and by choosing the right set of emotions, she was able to change the direction of her life.

Once Denise realized she had the authority to control her emotions, she began acting differently. Pushing aside feelings of resentment and self-pity, she became more supportive of her husband. Instead of sadness and depression, she chose joy and thankfulness. Her shift in mood and demeanor affected the atmosphere in her home and eventually the future of her children.

Years later, someone asked her oldest son Paul why he loves the ministry even though his dad was gone so much in those early days, and he acknowledged that Denise's attitude had greatly affected him while growing up. He said, "Because my mom was supportive of my dad, she taught us to be supportive of him. We felt like we were part of what he was doing."

Denise had no idea that her decision to take authority over her emotions was going to have that kind of influence over her children. She was simply putting the brakes on resentment, anger, jealousy, and depression and embracing the fruit of the Spirit. But as a result of her obedience, her children grew up with healthy attitudes toward their parents and toward the ministry.

Like Denise, we all have an opportunity to examine our emotions and take control of the direction our thoughts and feelings take us. We can choose fear, depression, or self-pity, or we can choose to live in the fruit of the Spirit. No one else can make that choice for us because we are each responsible for our own thinking, responses, and actions.

Thankfully, we also have the power of the Holy Spirit present within us. With His help, we can soar on those wings of authority and put the brakes on anything that might be a negative influence in our lives. When we wait upon the Lord, He infuses us with His strength so we can fly like an eagle!

STUDY QUESTIONS

Study to shew thyself approved unto God, a workman that needeth not to be ashamed, rightly dividing the word of truth.
— 2 Timothy 2:15

1. Isaiah 40:31 states, "But those who wait on the Lord shall renew their strength; they shall mount up with wings like eagles." What difficulty have you overcome with the help of God's supernatural strength in your life?
2. What obstacles did Queen Esther have to overcome in her life to accomplish God's plan?
3. Isaiah 54:2 states, "Enlarge the place of your tent, and let them stretch out the curtains of your dwellings; do not spare; lengthen your cords, and strengthen your stakes." What areas of your life has God instructed you to expand?

PRACTICAL APPLICATION

But be ye doers of the word, and not hearers only, deceiving your own selves.
—James 1:22

1. Can you think of a time in your life when God's supernatural strength carried you through a difficult situation in peace and joy?
2. What adjustments has the Holy Spirit prompted you to make recently?

3. Take a moment to examine your recent emotions. Are you choosing a set of negative emotions, or are you choosing the fruit of the Spirit?

LESSON 4

TOPIC

Endurance Is the Holy Spirit With a 'Thumbs Up'

SCRIPTURES

1. **Isaiah 40:31** — But those who wait on the Lord shall renew their strength; they shall mount up with wings like eagles, they shall run and not be weary, they shall walk and not faint.
2. **James 1:4** — But let patience have its perfect work, that you may be perfect and complete, lacking nothing.
3. **Philippians 1:9** — And this I pray, that your love may abound still more and more in knowledge and all discernment.
4. **Romans 5:5** — Now hope does not disappoint, because the love of God has been poured out in our hearts by the Holy Spirit who was given to us.
5. **1 Samuel 17:28-30** — Now Eliab his oldest brother heard when he spoke to the men; and Eliab's anger was aroused against David, and he said, "Why did you come down here? And with whom have you left those few sheep in the wilderness? I know your pride and the insolence of your heart, for you have come down to see the battle." And David said, "What have I done now? Is there not a cause?" Then he turned from him toward another and said the same thing; and these people answered him as the first ones did.
6. **1 Samuel 17:34-36** — But David said to Saul, "Your servant used to keep his father's sheep, and when a lion or a bear came and took a lamb out of the flock, I went out after it and struck it, and delivered the lamb from its mouth; and when it arose against me, I caught it by its beard, and struck and killed it. Your servant has killed both lion and bear; and this uncircumcised Philistine will be like one of them, seeing he has defied the armies of the living God."

SYNOPSIS

The Bible promises that those who wait upon the Lord will run and not grow weary and will walk and not faint. With the help of the Holy Spirit, we can run our race with endurance — even in the midst of the most challenging situations. We can also walk by faith daily, which includes loving others with God's love. By relying on the strength of God, we will be empowered to accomplish our purpose in life!

The emphasis of this lesson:

Endurance and faith are two key elements in our walk with God. Like the apostle Paul, we can learn to patiently endure difficult situations by maintaining an attitude of joy. We can also learn a lesson of faith from David, who didn't back down from his assignment even in the face of opposition. As we wait upon the Lord, we will soar like eagles, run without growing weary, and walk without fainting.

Running With Endurance

Let's look once again at Isaiah 40:31: "But those who wait on the Lord shall renew their strength; they shall mount up with wings like eagles, they shall run and not be weary, they shall walk and not faint." In the previous lesson, we discussed the divine design of the eagle and how God created it to gather strength and soar above the winds. Now, let's focus on the last part of the passage that exhorts us to run and walk. Whether we are flying, running, or walking, God is right there with us, giving us the strength to endure. In fact, His strength is perfect in every situation!

Perhaps you are in a busy season of life right now. Maybe your schedule is hectic and full of many responsibilities. All this activity may be requiring you to run in order to keep up with the pace of life. But thankfully, you don't have to do it alone. The Spirit of God lives on the inside of you, and He is there to give you the strength you need as you wait on Him.

In those running seasons, we are building endurance and patience in the midst of the pressure. James 1:4 says, "But let patience have its perfect work, that you may be perfect and complete, lacking nothing." This kind of patience actually means *endurance* — it is the ability to continue pressing forward without giving up. This special enduring power can only come from the Lord, and it is there to help us finish our assignment in times of adversity.

The apostle Paul is a great example of someone who exemplified endurance in his life. When he wrote the book of Philippians, he was imprisoned in Rome and living in extremely horrible conditions. Historians say that the prison was filled with rats, sewage, darkness, and death. Yet, in the midst of all these surroundings, Paul composed a letter to the Church that focused on joy. In fact, the book of Philippians records the words *joy*, *rejoicing*, and *joyful* 19 times!

Because his ministry was still needed, Paul chose to press through the difficult circumstances around him. He knew he hadn't completed his assignment, and that was why he chose to endure adversity with patience and joy. And as a result, the Holy Spirit infused him with supernatural power to press through the hardship and finish his race.

Like the apostle Paul, you can also choose endurance in the difficult seasons of life. You can push through hardships to victory because of the power of the Holy Spirit living inside you. He will help you run your race without growing weary!

Walking By Faith

Isaiah 40:31 also promises that God's strength can help us walk without fainting. Throughout the course of our day, we need supernatural strength to walk through challenging situations or even to deal with difficult people. Thankfully, we can practice walking by faith and not by sight on a daily basis.

One thing we need, especially in our walk of faith, is the ability to love others. In Philippians 1:9, Paul wrote, "And this I pray, that your love may abound still more and more in knowledge and all discernment." Through the power of the Holy Spirit, our love can continue growing every day. It can be bigger today than it was yesterday and bigger tomorrow than it is today. We can love people in the midst of the most challenging situations because God's love has been shed abroad in our hearts.

God's love in us can be like a constantly overflowing fountain. Our progress in this love will enable us to have the proper response to others in even the most difficult times, and as we learn to walk by faith daily in God's love, we won't fail in loving others. We won't give up on them and we won't quit them because we are just walking by faith every day.

A key attribute of walking by faith is not to be governed by physical perception. The Bible says we walk by faith and not by sight, so in other words, we believe what God's Word says about a situation even if we can't see it with our natural eyes or feel it with our natural senses.

For example, when Jesus appeared to the disciples after the Resurrection, Thomas was having a hard time grasping the reality of the situation. He literally had to feel Jesus' nail-scarred hands before he could believe it was Him. Jesus then later admonished him, "…Blessed are those who have not seen and yet have believed" (John 20:29).

Of course, the Bible is full of people who chose to believe God's promises even though they couldn't see what they were believing for with their natural eyes. They didn't give up on the word they received from the Lord, and they continued walking by faith one day at a time. And because of their steady faith, they were eventually rewarded with the physical manifestation of their promise.

David's Walk of Faith

Perhaps one of the greatest examples of walking by faith is King David from the Old Testament. Many years before God ever appointed him king over a nation, David began his walk of faith as a young shepherd boy. While keeping watch over his father's flock, he defeated both a lion and a bear. By the time the giant Goliath threatened the Israelites, David's faith was strengthened, and he was ready to fight and conquer this powerful Philistine!

However, when David arrived on the battlefield ready to tackle the giant, his oldest brother began to mock him, saying, "…Why did you come down here? And with whom have you left those few sheep in the wilderness? I know your pride and the insolence of your heart, for you have come down to see the battle" (1 Samuel 17:28).

David could have easily become offended or discouraged by his brother's words and attitude, especially since his brother was an authority figure in his life. But instead of letting those negative words discourage him, David just tuned him out and turned away. He kept going toward the word God had placed in his heart.

Sometimes, in our walk of faith, we encounter others who may belittle or mock us. They might not be supportive of our dreams and may not even care about us or have our best interest at heart. But no matter how others treat us, we must keep walking by faith toward the promise of God. We can't become weary in doing what God has asked us to.

After David turned away from the negative attitude of his brother, he had to face derision from another person of authority — King Saul! In this case, David didn't turn away — he spoke up boldly and said, "Your servant has killed both lion and bear; and this uncircumcised Philistine will be like one of them, seeing he has defiled the armies of the living God" (1 Samuel 17:36). David was certain of his ability in God to take that giant down!

Like David, there may come a time when we have to speak to our opponents and declare God's victory. When others come along and tell us we will never succeed, we may have to turn around and speak up to them. But by our speaking and declaring God's victory, we are agreeing with the Spirit of God. This simple practice can prevent us from fainting in our daily walk of faith.

As we wait upon the Lord, He will strengthen us for the journey ahead. He will cause us to soar over our problems like the eagle. He will impart endurance to us so that we can run and not grow weary, and He will empower us to walk and not faint. What a powerful promise! With the help of the Holy Spirit inside us, we can finish our race and accomplish all that God has planned for us.

STUDY QUESTIONS

Study to shew thyself approved unto God, a workman that needeth not to be ashamed, rightly dividing the word of truth.
— 2 Timothy 2:15

1. Isaiah 40:31 says, "But those who wait on the Lord shall renew their strength; they shall mount up with wings like eagles, they shall run and not be weary, they shall walk and not faint." How has waiting on the Lord helped you continue walking and running in your spiritual race?
2. The book of Philippians records the words "joy," "rejoicing," and "joyful" 19 times. Take a moment to locate all these verses in Philippians and then underline them in your Bible. Which verse speaks to you the most?

3. Paul wrote in Philippians 1:9: "And this I pray, that your love may abound still more and more in knowledge and all discernment." Now is a great time to examine how well you are loving other people. Are you allowing God's love to grow in your life daily?

PRACTICAL APPLICATION

But be ye doers of the word, and not hearers only, deceiving your own selves.
—James 1:22

1. What situations have you experienced that required you to endure hardships with patience?
2. What situations have you experienced that required you to walk in faith by practicing showing God's love to someone else?
3. What situations have you experienced that required you either to turn away or speak up in the face of mockery, scorn, or derision?

Notes

Notes

Notes

Notes

Notes

www.ingramcontent.com/pod-product-compliance
Lightning Source LLC
LaVergne TN
LVHW012034160826
845678LV00013B/2590